FUGUE AND STRIKE

Fugue and Strike

by Joe Hall

Black Ocean
Boston · Chicago

Black Ocean
P.O. Box 52030
Boston, MA 02205
blackocean.org

Cover Art and Design by Janaka Stucky | janakastucky.com
Book Design by Taylor D. Waring | taylordwaring.com

ISBN: 978-1-939568-67-0
Library of Congress Control Number: 2022948681

FIRST EDITION

Printed in Canada

TABLE OF CONTENTS

From People Finder Buffalo

1

Can't dream the economy because is good they might repo
          the economy your bed
is good can't dream because the economy is they might repo your good
dreams they economy is can't dream because you good the had the
bad to get a second economy to make rent the

that the body dream can be free—where all economies somebody
are free—the common, common
in that freedom, economy communion only dream in that
repo freedom in that freedom repo could only be—

2

Carl P, Ki Ki, hangs at J.T's fungus
mouth, J.T.'s normy horror
value cube urban slash J.T.'s Carl Paladino hangs out at
the dismal horizon of stage 4 Italian gentroids
you can. you can. 905 Elmwood. barfight.

3

Tim Howard arrests Tim Howard for murder
and spends the night looking the other other way
as Tim Howard knocks Tim Howard's head against
the hardness of the Erie County holding center
whispering, *murderer, murderer, murderer.*[1]

1   As of August 3, 2020 thirty people have died in the Erie County
Holding Center under Sheriff Tim Howard. Many died under suspicious cir-
cumstances (i.e. guards murdered them): Nathan Frailey, Daniel McNeil, Mar-
lon Clay, Michael G. Roberts, Joseph Balbuzoski, Robert J. Henchen, Joann
L. Jesse, John Reardon, Marguerite Arrindell, Adam Murr, Daniel Nye, Jeremy
Kiekbush, Keith John, Rakim Scriven, Trevell Walker, Lester J. Foster, Kristian
Woods, Edward Berezowski,, Patrick Yale, Richard A. Metcalf Jr., RosieLee
Yvette Mendez, David Liddick, India Cummings, Vincent Sorrentino, David
Stitt, Michael J. Girard, Joseph E. Bialaszewski, Connell Burrell, Daniel Spico-
la, Robert Ingalsbe.

5

The Allentown Association finds Allentown too queer, trans, butch,
and nonbinary and lodges a zoning complaint to evict
Allentown from Allentown so Allentown can quietly
be plaque in a dead, appropriately affluent organ.

7

Officer Tedesco stops Officer McAlister outside of
his house in Kenmore, his house from
which an American flag flies with one blue bar.
Officer Tedesco demands Officer McAlister
stop and show him his hands.
Officer Tedesco then beats Officer McAlister within
an inch of his life so Officer Parisi, who
was circling Mang Park, steps out
of his vehicle and shoots
Officer Tedesco 38 times.
Officers Parisi & McAlister write a false report at the station.
Officer Tedesco files a false report in hell.
Narcotics detective Joseph Cook, during a drunk
no-knock raid on the police station, stumbles and kills officers
Parisi & Tedesco. They are all thrown
a parade by the Minister of Flies.
All the people come to lick their shining leather
while the chief of police reads collaborative fiction.
Applause.[2]

---

[2]   Buffalo Police Officer Justin Tedesco killed Jose Hernandez-Rossy
as he fled. Hernandez-Rossy was unarmed. Read more: http://buffalonews.
com/2018/02/01/no-criminal-charges-against-police-in-fatal-black-rock-shoot-
ing/.

Officers McAlister and Parisi killed Wardel Davis after an unwarranted stop.
Read more: http://www.dailypublic.com/articles/05312017/why-meech-was-
stopped

Narcotics detective Joseph Cook "was single-handedly responsible for more dog deaths than all the reported incidents in the New York City in 2011–2012 alone." Over one three year stretch Cook shot and killed 25 dogs. Read more:http://www.dailypublic.com/articles/11152017/animal-killings-continue-dog-buffalo-police

FUGUE & FUGUE

FUGUE 1 | W/LINE FROM XIE XIANG-NAN

Wheels of fog turning no fog or planet for red and purple
riparian wedge of regressing where *production soaks production* in
the middle of a lateral captioned follicle tense wheel
turning, mauve jet does not soak production in the middle
of money immunized dome stapled apples with dimples rippled
intaglio clamor amor or phased dilation wheels turn fog
glimpse through oxygen or metonymic ice floe, this chain requires the
previous chain to say I am not a chain, heavy upon no fog or planet no

FUGUE 3 | FIREBALLS

"Labour out of control" sealing worker silence
friends w/babies, the organization of organizations, the organization
       of babies
management quotes, fireballs, friends w/babies, fireballs, worker
       silence, fireballs
the fireballs of organization, the organization of fireballs,
       friends w/fireballs
fireballs w/babies, "labor out of control," take the money or
       take the fireballs
fireballs of fireballs, faffs ff firefaffs, The Fireball Zone #3

FUGUE 6 | JACKED DADS OF CORNELL

Jacked Dads of Cornell are in the spirit door, the star door, where, Lo,
      long I walk
through the valley of food and all that food, multiplying in the sphere,
      to become a poet
is to a kill a poet, cling to a poet
in the last hour, before slipping into the drift
atoms of talk bounce in cylinders down Green St, predictive tongue
in the aleatory frame stream of vaticides
in the valley of food, jacked dads of Cornell blowing warp whistles
tech bros seduced into a sort of almost graspable
grammar, pleasure without vulnerability, rob them, rob them
      totally, leave them
drifting tongueless before the pulp vs. the throne, that's the title of
      Carrie Lorig's book, the title
of this poem, the fugue, The Fugue Zone #6: Jacked Dads of Cornell

FUGUE 7 | WHOEVER YOU ARE

Now that I work 6 days a week, I'm afraid of my thoughts on
the 7th, snarl and fragment, word easy
as a picture, hold a folder

like verdigris magma of eleven planets might slouch
out burning my feet through the floor
your crystallography of English words is a bust of the emperor

come with me, to the curb
whoever I am, our books
hit the pulper, our links go down

our names buried deep in the results where no one drills
friends remember we wrote but not what
we won't be remembered at all

that ticket to eternity lost
as we take death bed selfies then shyly touch the end
toasted orange, bubblegum, lime, ruby, taupe

redder draped look, particular mist, stitch touched, armamental search
wheel of fog turning, tense wedge regression
spore hatched sky slag through metal stencils

aleatory frame stream, eternity
the wrongest thing
The Fugue Zone 7

rhymes w/
The Fugue Zone Vol #8: Buffalo Free Rapid Transit

FUGUE 8 | BUFFALO FREE RAPID TRANSIT

Plot outside suffering on the apron of a well-worn grid, tense / wheel of regression, form drapes fog / planets, ride w/the breathing and plot, dead outside of crisis, touch stitches a wheel of spores, / riding with futures flowered from the aroma of a covered dish steadied in the cars' swarm by warm / fingers of milk, Fugue Zone Vol #8 subtitle: contentment form drapes magnetic plates red ride / while isles list, there was a time I planned suicide like a long vacation, on the apron / of a well-worn grid, I touched the stitches / laced my world together, in the cars' sway / there was a time I was by the warm fingers of music, red magnetic planets, then I got on Fugue Zone #8: Buffalo Free Rapid / Transit, sat w/the embroidery, touched the stitches, felt the tip of something I could not see in me that trembles, / something solid as a molar that grows wings and pulls, roots ripping from plot outside of suffering, / gum of my body, Buffalo's isles lean in the stream, it left a socket with the breathing and present departed / on the train my apron dilated, my nipple opened, plot outside of suffering, a bee flew in, planets of fog / impulse walks, I could feel them in me, a comb, made honey, it would be a job / to know okay, The Fugue #8: BUFRAT, plot outside of suffering, pliable contentment

FUGUE 9 | LOWELL

Asleep in the stream, I ask you to hold my hand
but you touch my leg, my neck parts, so I could not hold your hand
in the dream in the crumpled Taco Bell wrapper of who will be our
        destroyer
flattening nazis, popping trolls, morning slips between the cheeks of
        sleep, steep
descent, hair streams wander through your water, the pipe of faces,
        mouths in
a sequence, open, or turned down, eyebrows open or eyes held level,
        there the world swirls in their
liquid, disappears into the well as you back-float in the lens of your
        bed and the room slowly blinks
holding its sex in a jar of oil below the conveyor belt of air
the fruit skins, snack wrappers, shoebox tissue drifting out of the door,
        a retinue minus the poems
the bread came wrapped in, the letters stirred into the coffee grinder,
        scalded at the bottom of a cup
of instant soup, sealed in the heaviness of one's self, the mineral stream,
        smell of clay, oxidation over
a nail salon in Lowell, I wake up, stumble downstairs, into the chill,
        quarter of a block, order eggs
and coffee to go from a woman with a frank, impassive look, she asks
        if I want a fried dumpling too
I say yeah, she was right from the beginning

FUGUE 11 | HELLO, MY SLEEP

Hello, my sleep, my dawn thing
milk welling in the eyes

of night—if you should let me
if 6 am should slice this

cannister, carry the egg of this thought
in its mouth through the colliding

fonts of sensoria—the eyes of night
open, it all leaks out

this sleep just a plane
on the polyhedron: sleep, our sleep

rising over the world

FUGUE 14 | REARTICULATED SPHERE

The sidewalk spreads along a curve given by a graph, given by
      a shoulder
of a world, of desire, the curve pursues the curve inward, you can't eat
      oil, can't
eat porn, cheap or free, I tried, the spreading curve, effigy of an
executive placing strikebreakers on a map, we lived on the slopes of a
giant snail shell, raised doves and ate their small eggs to save money,
all I had to do was work unto sadness until
the sphere rearticulated, the room just a room, still we'd wake up
      small and gray
and find honey bled all over the pillows, the comb had passed
      through us and the
city spilled on, out of the window

FUGUE 15 | POLITICS? RUH ROH!

Quest Diagnostics' search terms yank pleasure bunches off
whole desires lick into company; lick into union, maids,
  childcare workers,
homecare workers, milkers, pickers, sex workers, far from
  neoliberalism
the podcast, the void, I still want you, inside of lemons instead of work
some X for place in proximity to make life, an old woman
really digging in her nose on the bus, I do not mine this book
  for bricks
for the fortress of a thought, I read this b/c I drown, translate
  dig, drill,
and burn as stream union imagining a Rubik's cube of love
and fucking as an emissions free, relatively customer-owned
cooperative employee union, tomato pickers union, a dimensional
door between hostile workplaces, storm clouds boiling
urine twisted over this town for eternity, wet ash
peppers the output of the sea union, too educated for solidarity
union, the emperor's power to project a million false bodies
union, to slay and lick while he walks in his own sight, not
only spectacle, we wrestle muppets for him in our once and
  holy bodies
union, roll the dice again, watch number interact w/equation

/

dice workers', troll catchers', great union of unions' union
great union of scabs, prosecutors, and police
The Fugue Zone #15 union, union of that

FUGUE 20 | CONSUMER COOPERATIVE BOOKSTORE

Deskilled & vomiting gold fog
the register a factory, their words stepping
on the pedal of your tongue, e-mail
deskilled my tongue, how it could hover
with your raw parts
vomiting gold, vomiting gold
you bag a book, watch it go through the
bindery, pulp at both ends
on Monday the manager confiscated your
"N," on Friday your "O", you try
to say "No," there's just a scab
in the air, during the Friday rush you
think you are being eaten alive
by a pack of small dogs
on Monday, you realize that's too
dramatic, you're just a chew toy
for know-it-all adjuncts of the ruling class
which might be worse, anyway
you go to say this to your coworker
but you both end up vomiting gold.

FUGUE 21 | VOMITING GOLD

For our mist floor transition woke the hell in me, vomited gold and
        faith time
couldn't touch you, vomiting gold, cask of stars and baffling
        make-up, woke
each time wandering what am I doing, streaming mists, slack
        shifts, lurch
where did this gold come from, vomiting gold, it hurts

FUGUE 22 | ANGELS UNION NO. 23

First line: shut up and shut up or ok shut up: Fugue Zone #22
Angels Union No. 23, weeks of rolling waking: what it's like to be
an angel even needs protection from the boss, grieve mist
among the array of soft candles of fog, Title XV: total devastation
by the choirmaster among bunched staves, liquor-filled berries, the
pleasure of saying no to prepare for a no that dives through itself
to no bottom, the accordion-folded breakroom thru the work floors
of heaven, the sex ok but they were listening, negotiations
broke down w/the creator around new sensory organ issues,
how it would be gathered for pleasure the ocean's sheer surface
pulled w/light in solidarity like
the array of candles among weeks of rolling grievance
crystal sleet sheets of soft walls, curtains, they say
the boss, though The Angels Union No. 1
built this city, it's almost as a wind
picks up, just further away, w/rent
up enough to force a second job or fly
away, as you can, in the liquor between planets, the grief
smoke weed, planets, watch the body flood, pain float
and become a hum, a debate
in The Angels Union No. 23
The Fugue Zone #22

FUGUE 23 | I DESIRE OBLIVION, RHYTHM, BREAKFAST

I desire oblivion over pleasure, mistook desire or pleasure
      then mistook
oblivion for desire, automation for passion, coffee for desire, carrying
      a saucer of cereal
sinking in milk, silk ray of coffee and some horror
seen by many as a rational choice, automation as inevitable, the
      unpeeling petals
where a subject should be radiation, coffee, frittered desire
      over the void
markets rise as dead planets between our eyes
until the very end, analysts say, rays unfold from the terminus of rays
      as circles of gold
cream crosshatching each other in the coffee, pleasure like the rotten
styrofoam of a simile, production exceeded production, all targets
lost in the union of I don't know what but it's happening, coffee,
extinction, desire cascades arcades, barcades
barricades, I mean desire ruptures in the surfeit of itself,
      mercury coffee
forfeited velvet pivoted from prolepsis, zeppelins of void seen
as known, known as seen, is as will, the rhythm, breakfast
scrambles, reticulation, unguent, music, The Fugue #23

FUGUE 29 | I'LL TAKE MY PRIZE NOW

Don't know why I feel happy, don't like that I feel happy a star of fur,
a saw of blurs, the other

side of contentment a scrum of maggots in the marrow, arrow-thin
        way, warp
drop me down on the long gray table, unfeeling, no agon wagon

or mistward listicle where you mow green time that the blade warps

clouds blown across the bloodshot sky, the earth filing
the ocean's grievances, or unowned shore, warp, weft, weft, warp

why should anyone be happy in the knot of their life

pulled both ways: no avatar, no pipe, no warp
for when I think of you, egg of the world

sailing toward the lawnmowering wormhole of my mouth

my happiness is not happiness, how could it be
a song of blurs, fistful of burs, unfrozen way, The Fugue

#29, how could there be anything but thunder
hissing on a grill of stars, Joe Hall? a mirror rolls under—

FUGUE 30 | I'M SO TIRED GET ME OUT-TA HERE

Get me outta these cubic yards of hair, composted air, rent to no rent,
       the sun
I'm so tired I can't pack this bowl, make whole this day in the running
       steam of my
thigh, oatmeal-clogged, can't soak this bowl, a matrix, a mist, a
       calendar of dogs
stroking out en masse in Caesar Augustus' infinity pool, our last
       action in
the old union's name, I thought that was funny once, now I do not,
       man, I'm so tired
under a key-lime light, while you play someone else's
body as if it were the flute of my own, we could sing that
together, The Fugue Zone #30, tired, going on

FUGUE 35 | OVERPRODUCTION/REIN-TEGRATION

What can we do when this work that we hate is all we have between
us, you, who I desire, with whom all I can speak of to you is a
      stain spreading
between your life and mine and not whatever is beyond the firewalls,
      the canyons
of ice in which we count these hours

you say who counts these hours, whose attention winds like a
      golden thread
through the eyelets of each wind-filled moment of each
day—looking at regional and national bags of chips floating on the
shelves of CVS while your prescription gets filled, drowsy scrolling,
thinking, perhaps, you will finally glimpse the engine between
its permutations, how someone tells you no they cannot put that small
but persistent fire out, how you've learned to no longer feel this
as devastation

you say who counts these hours and I do not know, I do
not think anyone counts these hours, we all just know each other's
lives are mostly lost to the fact that each day
they start over, down similar paths, we know this
that whatever we are can't be counted, is inexplicable and strange

FUGUE 36 | PHOTOCOPY OF LIGHT AND WATER

I am naked and the beams of light of iron, the beams of music
      I thought were from below
from without, are in the column, my neck, the throb of an artery
you are sitting tired in a van, your red balls resting on the seat
whole notes billow, the wind fills the worlds
we are naked by the crescent of the tan shore and teal water
there was work here, a sail and beams, cobalt spillways
among the vans, we hand each other off, hold each
other as the waves and irrelevance of buildings
blue, deep, and blue, is this something
the fugue could do?

FUGUE 37 | LATERAL WHEN

Fugue, all you said we could do was dodge through
one more day, without hurting someone
in our panic looking out into the ventricles of the city
the spirals and eyelets, the long-fingered clasp
days passed like rain or vapor from the dryer
where you put before us a meal, a steaming
tray, heaped with the future
and knuckles of egg, a thin slice
from the flame, would I say I was
deskilled in a long now of stocking shelves
would I say I had misplaced so much life
the sun breathes, massive, obliterating
who knew how to hold themselves
how to hold their own ache, who knew
the oil of fugue in a bottle cap by the fan
the laces of bus routes in the grievance file of heaven
there it is, there it always is
the Fugue Zone, the Fugue Zone #37

FUGUE 38 | BUFFALO FREE RAPID TRANSIT II

Someone published The Fugue Zone #8 Buffalo Free Rapid Transit,
    so here
is Fugue 38 Buffalo Free Rapid Transit between
the moons that separate us, chewed almost translucent
fingernails, for the transit would take us even though the
spine of our house was twisted, still we went, had to go
and find a seat that would accompany our infirmities
buying lumber at 2 am, the cut and remainder
you asked me what poetry could be
Buffalo Free Rapid Transit's tracks river the mirror, riddle
the mayor and stops shuffle, backtrack, the knight's move
through Forestlawn, for you see the legislation
it'd also have to convey the dead who were for so long
stranded, bags in the snow

FUGUE 40 | DEBT AFTER DEBT

I consider debt after debt, a gold flare
at a tiny intersection in the mammoth complex
of my femur, debt, though, whole notes
consuming the bar, any silence it had left
drives down I-90, ribbons of rain splattering
on wipers, drive for an hour
to work for who, to pay off who
I consider debt, each word, each poem
an easter egg, w/absence inside and inside absence
you are hunger, breathing this time and value
particularized into mist, you are there, at the end
of another shift, the Fugue Zone #40
interest and endless tho you
blind me, I don't know to die

FUGUE 41 | LAID OFF AT A CANNABIS GROW, UPSTATE NEW YORK

Mist pebbles plastic sheeting the hoop house
grid, pot doubles us over seed
tray tables, wraps our backs in
fists of stressed muscles and squeezes, seeds
spill, volunteer hemp climbs and genders unsupervised
time clock apps, gas station lunches, and Knightlight's
ship that is a fungus threaded through its crew
a game they carry in their mind
before we all get fired on a whim
but leave our technique behind
for some beard in raybans
who wishes his phone were a gun, sun
drops on green hands pressed by paychecks
to oil, The Fugue Zone, The Fugue Zone #41
dropped on green hands grown into green hands
crushed into oil

FUGUE 42 | FIREBALLS II

Fireballs, pastel squares and snails
snares, fireballs of asters, pastors'
mouths wrapped around one hundred
flowers' green stems, fireballs, balls
of fire and fire, the world is not
fire just fireballs as liars and liars
of fireballs that peel this dome of rain away
pearl of wet rivulets you could
call yours in a trail down the plate glass
and I could drink a beer in the natural light
of 2013 like a salamander under
a rock and you could zip the fireball up
around you, the house would burn
you'd be the same and I'd still be left
trying to think of the title of the Frank
O'Hara poem with the beautiful slope
of urine and someone banging on metal
and fireballs and mist though
I'm trying to be over Frank
there he is in my stupid brain
like a thigh-like slope of urine
and banging on a piece of rebar in a dream
which is often the only information
that matters, wholer than
a whole note, the seed of fire

in a rope of saltwater slung
window to window where you lived
in 2009 in Baltimore in
Fugue Zone #42
broom of an aster
kept the pay stub but not
the pay, not the damp matches
or broken chemistry and fireball
is replaced in the store window
by some other thing, some
other thing, not even chiasmus
could do anything with
fireball's cold dust
thin film, crumbling mist
snails and pastel squares
I don't remember you
I just remember that I don't
remember you, The Fugue Zone
The Fugue Zone #42

FUGUE 43 | VETIVER, RETWEETED LAVENDER

Vetiver, retweeted lavender, truly
spreading flock of colors on the
tender spring hills, I walk naked
with the tax exemptions of the lord
retweeted log rotten with honey, stuffed
w/music, chamomile, and flax
it cost me nothing to walk with
the stream there as someone plucked a string
strapped against a comb of wood
retweeted lavender, tax-exempt
and a totally chill covenant
under a chevron of clouds

FUGUE 47 | SOME KINDA GRAIL PROBLEM

Lamp, the flowering column, in the mist, in the axiom, you sit
in your red armor, the loose prism that peels light from light
in moon-smashed foil, playing your cards on a
table of mist, we are in those cards
mothers, tyrannicides, mechanics
you hold the city like a puzzle box to your ear
in the moon-smashed mist, fingers testing
its surfaces, red armor under
a flowering tree split by honeyless bees
in a cold summer, rivers of cellophane, and a desire
that's real, to choose between signs suspended
among vegetation made out to be tragic, lamp, flowering
column, drunk cask of lights, or the red armor
cross-legged under the jungle gym
mothers, tyrannicides, and mechanics
great alabaster hull of a planet
great honeyless planet
great planet of smoke

FUGUE 48 | UNSAINTED, UNKINGED, W/A LINE FROM J. MILTON

Unkinged fog, leftovers in foil
you poured love, like salt, over all that
anger and asked us to eat, an ache
balled in the sleeve of today will you
ask me to massage away, a hernia
in the sun's fabric, new bills grow
between the cracks of contract jobs, new flags
of carbs to quilt the squirm of these thoughts
at the door with a game in a bag
healed by an ordinary saint
undebted, unkinged
in the leftovers, the latecomers, the fog

who kills a king must kill him while he is king
who kills a king must kill him while he is king
who kills a king must kill him while he is king
who kills a king must kill him while he is king
who kills a king must kill him while he is king
who kills a king must kill him while he is king
who kills a king must kill him while he is king
who kills a king must kill him while he is king
who kills a king must kill him while he is king
who kills a king must kill him while he is king
who kills a king must kill him while he is king
who kills a king must kill him while he is king

FUGUE 49 | THEORIES OF CHANGE

The Fugue Zone #49, make it to 50, soggy shovel-face of printouts
cascade of cascades around the sun, who drank fog through a
      bone-straw
who dawned in extinction and dawned in cascades of extraction
whose mist of money and dollars, value an hour and an anti-aesthetic
beating its head against the wall, don't let these letters spell hope
in blistering paint in the sucked-dry colleges of the state
where we gotta seize each other before the rotten white-messiah
mask permanently grafts onto the face, what thing
makes one sing, how to change, deftly, away
from this heavy traffic of mist, tolling of bells, growl of
letters, The Fugue Zone #49, time and time some more

FUGUE 50 | FUGUES 1-50

Vomiting gold in a turning wheel
where production soaks production
no memecade can surpass, wheels

of turning fire, fogs echo in the spheres
trilobites pour through metal stencils
jacked dads of Cornell blow warp whistles

to uproot lives to starmaps they can read
an aleatory frame stream, Buffalo's isles
lean in the flow over

a nail salon in Lowell, I wake up, stumble
this fiction explodes my baby meat
falls below styrofoam comets

milk wells in the eyes of this AI sun
this hostile workplace mist lime hums
the sidewalk spreads, all we have to do is work

unto sadness in the fossil tide
of nerves flaring through cell walls
brittle webs of mist, an engine heavy

enough to haul off what you know
vomiting gold during the Friday rush
between the sliding calipers of mist

weeks of rolling waking in the union
of I don't know what has
someone shot off your jaw and

put the joystick down?
was it a rosy kiss or hand or toilet
that rose out of the ground?

in the net of their life, w/the knots
pulled twice, oatmeal-clogged undertow
key-lime lights, staph-infections, tomorrow

flaming trains flung into the roundhouse
you say who counts these hours, I do not know
whose whole notes billow

into the ventricles of the city
debt after debt
find a seat for our damage, absence

inside and inside absence
fists of stressed muscles squeeze
you could call your own in a trail

down the plate glass
driving to my second job
under the swelling yolk of the sun

in this mist, the axiom, drunk cask of lights
a hernia in the fabric where new bills grow
don't let these letters see

don't stop vomiting gold

FUGUE 62 | THE HOUR OF LIFE IN WHICH MISTAKES BECOME APPARENT

Fireballs, poem w/history, vortex, lockdown
double column or circumambient arc of flame
shatter, ocean, time, you grinder, thrush
brush, abrasive, abrazos, let us go
like D. LeMay says, what if we
could start again
in the cheap seats where nobody cares
if you stand for the anthem
(Mayer? Waldman?) as a trepanned
dome, gold flakes blown
onto the brain's soft working tissue
the wild atmosphere's radius
touches the mind, if we could start again
shotgunning hand sanitizer or huffing emerald dust
if I have said fireballs, I meant you
if I have said garden, I meant a wet
biochemical weave of mycelia and roots walled
from arguments about property and the lyrical
working self, if I have said I've wasted
my life in poems, I meant today is day
41 of lockdown, waste is a
form of devotion, to what, to who
the answer is not the Fugue Zone
or fireballs, or the Fugue Zone #62

FUGUE 65 | SESTINA ZONE

I am crossing the bridge of my life,
The Fugue Zone: a haired spine of bone

comets across the knife of the night
where what is on the other side

lies open like a bloody egg
of mist. Kiss me through this mask,

and if in bed I should wear the mask
if you should mistake my life

for a mask cratered like a bloody egg,
feathers, yolk, blue-black eye and bone,

you'll turn away, onto your side
to wake with a siren cross-hatching the night

of crocus teeth huddle among indigos. Night,
long-salted lime, take off your mask.

I want to see your two scarred faces, side
by side, and kiss them both. Yolk of life,

let's linger here. Later still,
hold in your mouth the robin's egg

the world's great turning gear, fermenting
flood. If I were to count each night

like a torn punch card, a bone that will not glow—
if this long night were to drop its mask,

you would be there, beside my sleep, your life
revolving around tomorrow, beside

me. Can worry become bread? I turn on my side,
hungry. We are twins of the egg

in a roving quarantine,
this delicate bridge: night.

Who can read it? Reach for my braille mask
touch the thought hovering above bone,

read the forefinger as it travels over bone
as our bed skates night's glass. Which side

are we on as dark ice implodes and
our bodies burn nearing the last egg

of each letter like gasoline—night:
our double wakes clasping the other's life

in The Fugue Zone's glittering mask of bone
where our life devours our lives inside

this softly cooking egg of night.

FUGUE 66 | BLUE & BLUE

1.
The long fugue of my life, no point, against my life, eros, friends,
        mutiny, the miracle
of travel, got this scratch above the woodshop, spinning blade
drill, screw, and chop, mutiny, round as a robin on a lip split ship
no silos of angels and lumber, what's this but liquid like sanitizer,
        mutiny on the
lumber, barge and frame, can't live in it, maybe through it, your
generous pour
of spittle, mumble lumbered letters in innumerable, what a kid would
        do is chuck
this grid at the wall like a rotten apple, though you know the bruise
        is there
to feed the seed, chain links there to flower, there for the tongue to
swim in spring
against my life, eros, friends, mutiny against the sonnet,
        abecedarian, or ode
or crust of a note, mouse curled inside, this fatigue, this union w/
        strange dues
underwrites a mole-work rhythm that crosscuts this maze
violence made, displacement, memory bleed—against the
        buttonwood tree
in the gauze caked in to scab this wound who feels never stopped
unwrapping, the long fugue whose life the fog lifts what remains
is the gasoline at the center of our signature, what remains
is our want, a tongue and cracked tooth to gnaw at the knot

2.
Would a mastodon open its green grinding jaw and call through the
        museum, call
through the studs, though the web of pipes, drains, and wires
this fugue has outlasted days, confusion, trying to peg
a mind w/memory, resolution and who will find an angel
in the stifling heat, is not protection, a pus column, sacrosanct
and sign-posts whiffle, can't drive roads forking
night, car peeling apart under the eye of the huge oceanic mammal
        I want
to patrol my dreams or love letters written in the clatter
of hammers, constant repair of wood quitting wood, the new moon's
most light this day will ever get, that's beyond fine
shed words not repetition like the wheel rolling is also a drum
also called following you, walking along, plum-wired storm
from safety at the bottom of stasis, fear
stale drugs ground into the rug yet always, always numerous

3.
Did I name saints or silos, did I name desire, did I name rent, did I
name unemployment, that story, that stent, waking blue
        by the window
wondering whether to ask for another cure to the splits in my life
and if there were a train that silently stood beside your door,
        would it matter
where it took you but that it could, so a metaphor for us and
        some country

not named death, you said this all takes money, if money has
        taken everything
it should give it back, in the yellow field, the flash and scatter
of photovoltaic cells and rent strikes, without light, a candle
as the wind sweeps over the Niagara, plummeting heaven
what's left, in our bed, and have I reached for you, have you
        reached, those
shrinking territories of our bodies where touch is still a comfort
what's left in the function of the melody, the dust flying notes
rearrange, when has this duration become pain and is there
another side, debtless to this oil pressed from
from the sleeve of our sleep, softness, the state of
this fugue for the unknown, for emergence, for who

FUGUE 76 | WHEELS

We had to bike down Rohrer for the plant burger, we had to see the
      long legs
of the man flung out from his chair in the green shady lawn
      of a derelict
house down the giant wounded sycamores of Rohrer
you said you weren't working by the fountain saucer
of MLK park, biked by TVs that blew their brains out, masked
and 6 ft apart on a bench, rhubarb chutney, sorrel
spelling out with your hands a soil delivery, this is on
the cross-town train, the sunlit fog, the mist bleeds bread
TVs w/their brains smashed out, in the reborn green, dumplings
w/dumpster-dived pork, was it a clarinet or an accordion
softly pressed, cars streaming weed inside the crisis
anger and a reflective ease down the worn-out houses of Rohrer
beans and roasted cauliflower in the train
the blue tracks that run under the crumbling, down
into olive oil where black-eyed peas swim, bread and bike wheels
the pea of mist bleeds bread, practice and naïve or easy fix
The Fugue Zone, The Fugue Zone #76

FUGUE 87 | WHERE WE CAN WALK W/GRIEF

How could this poem be the hair of a tree
sunglare leaking from whose mouth, there will be no guarantees
when can I walk w/the grief, where the grief sours
my lips that had been wet w/yr kiss

and have I been kissed, who was gathered in whose arms
you try to touch something in me, reach down, pull
what smooth rock moon from the mouth
of the stream, spit of rent, drip

not to swim but to turn in the wet cement, follow
the crest & breaking, I touch you, you
sink further into yourself, you dive in
after, like sun splits across water

FUGUE ZONE PROCESS NOTE | A LAN-GUAGE FOR EXHAUSTION

what can I write when I feel like each phrase is a soft shell
against the blast of a horn an angel blows to end the world
and there was R wearing a shift that said IRAN, IRAN
IRAN, IRAN while M reads his piece on Ronnie Spector
and J had us draw the lodger in our head, mine was a
knot of wrinkles telling me to burn this before
reading, there were things I was afraid to say
to these long friends, like I think the last six months
have taken something from us, some myth of how we
could be to ourselves, and what we have left is each
other, can you see how my poems could be a silver wash
of sympathetic noises, production quotas are
up at the black candle factory, and you keep
asking me how I am, the angel brings the horn
to his blood-sticky lips and we hold on

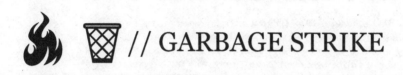 **// GARBAGE STRIKE**

BUFFALO & ITHACA, NY, USA
JAN–MAY 2019

Garbage Hurled At Police In Paris General Strike

Paris, June 19.—(Æ)—Garbage collectors heaved garbage at police and blocked a thoroughfare with their trucks in Paris today during a one-hour general strike called throughout France by the Communist-controlled general confederation of labor.

During the shutdown, the garbage collectors drove their trucks toward the plaza in front of the city hall. Police stopped them. The garbage men then began throwing garbage at the police and finally used their trucks to block traffic through the Avenue Victoria.

Police arrested some. When the symbolic walkout ended, the garbage truck drivers went back to their trucks and resumed work.

The strike protested police action Tuesday night in throwing rubber workers out of the Bergougnan tire factory in Clermont-Ferrand, where they were on a sitdown strike for a 20-cent pay rise.

* * *

employes, including h o s p i t a l workers, s t r u c k. White-collar workers remained at their desks but refused to work.

* * *

Most Paris policemen, however, stayed on duty. The majority are in Popular-Republican and workers' force syndicates.

Premier Robert Schuman received a delegation from the Popular Republican union and then conferred with Labor Minister Daniel Mayer.

DAILY NEWS INDEX

The United States war machine is the largest user of petroleum in the world. It murders even when idling its engine.

City of Toronto Dump Wagon, 7 March 1917.

For it is spilling and spilling from several terminals
for it is coming and here and coming
for that as long as we live and after
is a flood brimming to the lip
for it requires so much work
beyond planning piled
against the window the eyes crossing boundaries
to become its own life blooming
shit exuberant
thank you drain? thank you gravity? nope no no
nope no 1.3 kg matter, some fos.fuel into 2 g
microchip iPhone 22 chips
 a 12 yr old (JG Dig waste 26)
junk expresses beyond production
in exchange consumption
NOTE: STOP HUMPING RAGPICKER

(cont'd page 2) from THOUSANDS OF GARBAGE STRIKES,
THOSE DOCUMENTED, EASY TO FIND: New York, NY 1667;
Mumbai, India 1878; Toronto, Ontario 1918; Paris, France 1948; St.
Petersburg, FL, 1966; New York, NY, 1968; Memphis, TN 1968; St.
Petersburg, FL 1968; Miami, FL 1968; Lubbock, TX 1968; Cleveland,
OH 1968; Charleston, SC 1969; New Orleans, LA 1969; Oklahoma
City, OK 1969; Atlanta, GA 1970; London, Great Britain 1970;
Tokyo, Japan 1973; New York, NY 1975; Atlanta, GA 1977; Detroit,

MI 1978; San Antonio, TX 1978; Tuscaloosa, AL 1978; Philadelphia, PA 1986; New York, NY 1990; Toronto, Ontario 2002; Chicago, IL 2003; Athens, Greece, 2006; Vancouver, British Columbia, 2007; Naples, Italy, 2008; Seattle, WA with Columbus, OH with Buffalo, NY with Mobile, AL, 2012; Guangzhou, China, 2008, 2012-2013; Birmingham, UK, 2017; Paris, France, 2018. ABSTRACT: A work: to be w/ppl

w/multitudes, not take
shit Work an obsession
w/turning trash around
as tactic "Art must be destroyed
in order to not become
merchandise or an institutional icon" Heriberto Yépez

w/years work bad and failure
to fix it w/anyone go tho we try
dumb hope in my mouth

NOTE: STOP HUMPING RUINS

if this is trash
send it back
HERE IS SOME PROSE

1677

Dutch Amsterdam had become New York. New York City Dutch cartmen—waste carriers—become some of the first workers in the colonies to face punishment for striking. Initially, there was no division of labor for these carters. Carters hired themselves to carry any goods: lumber, dung, grain, felons to the gallows. Their 1667 contract with the city recognized that they were a "fellowship" that could fix rates. In exchange, the city required them to perform various municipal duties such as fighting fires, maintaining roads, and taking turns on Saturday afternoons carting household "dirt" to a dump for "ten stivers seawant." Carters became semi-official city workers in a waste market mediated by the colonial state.

Living in small dwellings in a back alley called Smith's street, they remained the poorest taxpayers in the city. New York's merchant oligarchy complained that the carters liked to drink, race their carts, turn down work, and offer insults.

Ten years into the contract, after a murky dispute, the mostly Dutch carters struck. In retaliation, the city fined the strikers 3 shillings or 15 loads of garbage to the wharf, suggesting part of their transgression was their refusal to haul shit. This same year, city officials passed a law barring black New Yorkers from carting or portering, though they could do so under the Dutch regime. Instead, white carters would employ Black New Yorkers to do the carter's job for a fraction of their wage. The same year the Dutch carters struck they received the wages of whiteness. This racial work hierarchy was also dependent upon a sort of city citizenship. Obtaining a carter license required one to be a freeman of New York. The city granted freeman status only after a certain term of residence. Though if one was a slave—and New York was a slave city—one was not a free man.

Paulo d'Angola, Simon Congo, Anthony Portuguese, and John Franciso. Some of the known names of individuals brought to Dutch New Amsterdam in 1625 or 1626 as slaves by the West India Company. These men were owned by the company and did company work for the benefit of European colonists and shareholders in the Netherlands. Company work often meant building and maintaining the proto-infrastructure of what would become New York City: walls, wood, stones, piers, roads. The back-breaking stuff of making permanent European occupation of Lenape lands.

In 1635 the company put an overseer on its books, Jacob Stoffelsen. In 1641 Stoffelson forced these men to pick up and haul off dead hogs from the streets. Slaves of the company-colony, forced to make settler life possible through the waste work of clearing the way. During the chaotic 1640s, it was not clear what happened to d'Angola, Congo, Portuguese, and Franciso, but what is clear is that in the ensuing decades, several Black residents of New Amsterdam joined the ranks of workers paid in wages to cart waste before their exclusion from the work in 1677.

For Dutch carters, the wages of whiteness wouldn't remain sufficient. New York's carters struck again in 1684 as part of a wave of unrest against a newly installed English, royalist administration intent on disciplining laborers, apprentices, servants, and slaves. The carters' source of pain was the administrative imposition of further public service requirements, including hauling goods to the colony's fort twice a week for free.

In response to the strike, the Common Council fired every carter. A week later, the council couldn't find replacements, hamstrung by their licensing system defined by city citizenship and anti-Blackness. In turn, the Common Council rehired the carters who struck.

Over the next century, carting became specialized with some carters working more often for the city to collect refuse. By the 1780s, the system had broken down. Carters more often than not refused to put in their customary days picking up people's shit. The Common Council turned to hiring private companies to remove "dirt" and allowing unlicensed individuals to get paid to haul trash.

By the early 19th century Irish immigrants made inroads into the carting business. This was met with resistance: there were fights in the streets between resident carters and immigrant Irish carters. By 1818, Mayor Colden compromised with carters who complained that Irish carters were encroaching on their turf. The Mayor's compromise: "Aliens henceforth would only be allowed to hold 'dirt carters' licenses; aliens were thus forbidden to engage in the more palatable and lucrative forms of carting."

Over two centuries, New York coupled harder lines between supply and disposal with the hierarchization of workers by race and citizenship. It repeatedly forced people of color and immigrants to perform the uncompensated or low-wage waste work on which the health of the colony's white residents depended. This is not to say the force applied to New York's Black residents, people of color, and Irish immigrants was at all equal or that these are monolithic categories. And this is not to mention the countless women who did much of the informal, unpaid initial work of disposing of household crud. They were always excluded from NYC's formal wage waste market.

By the time of the civil rights era, the public sector strikes, and the famous 1968 Memphis Sanitation Strike, in many cities most sanitation workers were Black or Latin American. The work was extremely dangerous and the workers were often paid less than living wages. Sanitation strikes followed in places like Tulsa, St. Petersburg, Charleston, and Lubbock. Those departments that were predominately Black tied their strikes to the civil rights struggle: with just pay, workers demanded an end to the "plantation mentality" of bosses. Many city officials granted pay raises while ignoring demands for respect.

Asbestos powdered to ink J said "a poison redistribution ethos"
w/the warmth of blue copper oxidized in vinegar

but whose hand gets to mix? the place no
one wants to be in but all can go Lone Star

tick as noble virus vector that makes meat an allergen if you
        got to *Hactenus*
Inculta the beings of power hitherto uncultivated by us where

the sovereign shall carry your shit
Waste value capitalism grinds the world

through the dialectical pair for their hell is a non-dialectical dust

For the island fortresses of financialization from which they
        liquidate the world
compacted from trash

commons reformed into plantation
The EZLN reference democratizing dust
Purity is trash What's a flow?

Carried

That waste esp in its most corrosive
forms can stay contained Slander

against all matter's nature
to drift tho this paper

thin lie allows management to leave
shits in the backyard

of the poorest For the dioxin
an I may be and lead an I

I am streams live for the
channel this I involves barf

rainbow my servers serve grade
F meat cache deposit of

being that can be a power w/yrs
garbage strike returns leachate

to the shitter's teeth
Corrupt as shit

Ferrous Bueller

2001

In the 1980s, Oaxaca City officials determined they would dump the city's waste on land carved out of communal holdings adjacent to the Guillermo González Guardalo neighborhood, on the city's periphery. This landfill performed a service for the residents of Oaxaca whose cost the members of Guillermo González Guardalo had to bear. Many began to suffer environmental illnesses from the trash of the city that denied them basic services such as electricity.

In January 2001, members of the neighborhood, sick of the city's refusal to clean up or remove the rapidly expanding dump, barricaded the dump's access road. Garbage trucks couldn't unload. Collection throughout the metro area ground to a halt.

In Oaxaca City, modernization produced an expectation of cleanliness but capitalist modernization also causes cities and suburbs to sweat waste at a tremendous rate. City residents could ignore protestors but not their own piling shit. As Sarah A. Moore puts it, "By forcing the citizens of the center to live with their own waste, [the residents of GGG] reverse their relationship to the abject and also, to some degree, challenge their own abject status."

And using garbage, no matter the use, risks that garbage sticking to the self in the social eye. So, in 2001, residents of Guillermo González Guardalo refused refuse. In the Oaxaca protests, the Popular Assembly of the Peoples of Oaxaca took over and ran the city. The right to the city was expressed through the practice of direct, democratic, and autonomous forms of governance.

Protests continue in Oaxaca, though hostile media has worked to metonymize protesters with trash. One 2018 NPR story lamented the disruption teacher protests represented to the city's booming restaurant industry, which caters mostly to Americans. It mentions that Oaxaca's biggest daily, *El Imparcial*, printed photos of what they said were piles of teacher trash. Following the lead of the impartial NPR, their "gritty" food blog, *The Salt*, implicitly sided against protesting teachers, reducing them to rubbish. Gringos gotta eat! While teachers lose sleep commenting on papers and planning protests and the good enough growth of hundreds of lives.

Throttle, tax, and deletions signal a throttle in the extrusion of data if its line of transmission were cut or if those sniffing the horde If I multiplied a billion-fold becoming a rotten packet could they choke in the act of eating tracks becoming rotten in its checkpoints Though Acxiom's or Clearview's stomachs virtually infinite could its throat distend and rupture or to dispose of one's feral trace to self-efface how much solidarity w/o solidarity would it take in the power fantasy a server farm craters w/a blackout w/a firehose.

AZ server farm churns the image of a tidiness personality blasts
fuel in tons burning to cool itself before collapse > extraction flood
hits thrift store That the other production of light
dematerialized distributes far beyond the horizon
I streamed the image of the moon hollowed out and then caving
in on its huge and heavenly self from the intake of the server farms
mined into its surface In a pinch policed
inventory becomes waste looters transform
to life The contents of my mouth butthole & colon
ATM for penthoused stranger CRT
monitor up to 8 lbs lead 2lbs copper desktop 620
lbs rock drill of the horizon for the island deep
sea for the continental shelf the asteroid
moon and lunar dust for the horizon the drill of the horizon
for the sublime is a scraping drill res extensa
is yr being yr being yr being & yr
being to them
Hired to take a bunch of shit from her acerbic boss
"your job to make X happy" records it
delivers the load Whole shifts
of my only life spent clicking
shit in the group inbox into the trash last in
first out no one else would bother
Will there be a beautiful city or ward
shitatoriums many gendered

and degendered, single and multi-stalled
spaces of beautiful excretion? Will there
be a space of public salvage and reclamation
and disassembly of the greatest machines of violence?
Will we celebrate the decommissioning and destruction
of pernicious things and institutions?
Will the work of disposal be in perpetual rotation
or purely elected? Redeem the hours spent
soaking someone's sour feelings
exporting memory an account in
bags of tumor-fertilizing sediment
w/clear labels re: vintage provenance
thick-bottomed tumbler w/alphabet
block-sized ice cube melting
in a cocktail of lead dioxin
ICE field offices flush their shit
Trump Towers flush their shit
The Westin Hotel fellow tenant of Buffalo's
ICE field office draping a point
of carceral intake with the façade of comfort
flushes its shit If we can't
separate ourselves from shit if we don't
involve it in some other process
we die If the rich can't
export their guilt past the gates of their community
if we don't let the execs out of the vacuum bag
if no trash left the police station, gated communities

if no trash left the board rooms of Silicon Valley
if no trash left the White House
or the last 3 bosses' offices
if all I do is talk

1684

Thomas Burnet's influential *Sacred Theory of the Earth* is one of the first geological conceptions of deep time. In it he writes "[the earth and moon] are both in my judgment the image or picture of a great Ruine, and have the true aspect of a World lying in its rubbish." In planetary ruin, nostalgia for a prior world: "We have still the broken Materials of that first World, and walk upon its Ruines." Burnet's longed-for world is the egg of Eden, perfectly smooth and symmetrical. All the world's water that would become seas, oceans, and lakes located within the egg's shell. Viewed from the present moment, Burnet's ideas appear to be bad and stupid. Yet his planetary catastrophism never died. It entered a cycle of white thought that redeemed and doomed the planet, moving from ontologies of universal God-smote matter to inert fragments awaiting the divine animation of the "human" touch, Whitman's *Leaves of Grass* to Eliot's Wasteland. Romantic conservation to capitalist "improvement."

Imaginations at the root of capitalist colonial empires want to kill the world by imagining it as killed. In this state of horror and optimism, they claim the right to possess the whole dead world, to process its body. The garbage-world is fundamental to the outlook of settler colonialism. Nick Estes on the destruction of Lakota lands via flooding created by post-WW II Pick-Sloan dams built by the Army Corps of Engineers: "Our lands, and lives, were targeted not because they held precious resources or labor to be extracted. In fact, the opposite was true: our lands and lives were targeted and held value because they could be wasted—submerged, destroyed."

If the whole world was a ruin, the dump could be anywhere, upon any other.

Romantic conservation, what would become in the United States settler conservation at its worst—denying the naturalness of open, changing systems, denying, also, the right and history of indigenous peoples in using and producing their landscape, folding them back into nature—produces aliens and invasive species while disappearing first peoples to get back to the egg, the Eden, a healthy colony for the colonist.

Edward Abbey was a piece of shit.

The world is not a ruin.

1971

The people of Tokyo's Kōtō ward carried out their own dump blockade.

At this time, Kōtō ward contained 2/3rd of the city's landfills, including the infamous Island of Dreams, a spreading landform of trash in Tokyo Bay. As their bay filled with trash islands, Kōtō ward residents became sick of the city using their home as a toilet. Their blockade was catalyzed by the Suginami ward's resistance to building its own trash incinerator. Suginami ward was large, populous, and wealthy. Luxe trash for Kōtō

In Eiko Maruko Siniawer's account, on December 22, 1971, Kōtō ward residents checked every truck that arrived at Landfill Number Fifteen and turned back those carrying Suginami's garbage. In May 1973, Kōtō ward assembly members again physically barred entrance to this dump. This confrontation was called "The Garbage War," also the name of a major sanitation program by Tokyo's mayor Minobe. The dump blockade likely occurred with the implicit approval of Minobe, for whom building ward incinerators was a marque project. If Suginami couldn't shit on Kōtō, then mayor Minobe might move Suginami to build their own incinerator. Still, it was Kōtō ward residents who put their bodies in front of garbage trucks to turn them back to the rich part of town.

1969

The Young Lords began the Garbage Offensive in East Harlem. They turned piles of garbage into a flaming blockade of Third Avenue and 111th Street to protest, among other things, what would now be called the city's environmental racism through unequal sanitation services. Through the construction of the spectacle of flaming garbage, The Young Lords and members of their community forced the matter, twisted the mayor's arm, and won better service. Which was not the only end.

The 1968 Memphis Sanitation Strike most often appears as the backdrop for Martin Luther King Jr.'s turn to labor militancy and his assassination. It was also notable for the violence the city met protestors with. This included cops and many members of the KKK killing sixteen-year-old African American Larry Payne. It was also part of a national wave of sanitation strikes that overlapped with a wave of civil service strikes.

1978: A turn. Ten years after Memphis' sanitation strike, the Memphis police and fire departments struck. A Memphis cop explained why: "I'm so tired of feeling like a garbage man." Memphis' Black sanitation workers had just won a new contract. Middle-class and overwhelmingly white, these cops could not articulate their desire for respect outside of racial hierarchy. How this officer described his condition makes clear he was striking for the wages of whiteness. And that he could only express solidarity with Memphis' sanitation workers in the most back-handed way.

During the Memphis police and fire-fighter strike, polls showed that white Memphis did not support these striking municipal unions. However, the same polls showed that Memphis' Black community supported them in spirit. That was as far as their support could extend. Despite repeated appeals for AFSCME's members in the sanitation department to conduct a sympathy strike, the Black community refused to mobilize on behalf of the police union, whose members were often their oppressors. Eventually, white unionists would turn to coercion with firefighters picketing city sanitation facilities. Almost no sanitation workers crossed these pickets, some stating they didn't cross for fear of violence from firefighters.

The Memphis cop strike was part of a cop strike wave that was, in part, a reaction against sanitation workers' wins. New Orleans, 1979: Cops strike twice. Mardi Gras events are canceled for the first time since WWII. This was a decade after a New Orleans sanitation worker strike. Officers professed to feeling "humiliated" that sanitation workers won a collective bargaining agreement with the city when they hadn't. In 1969 garbage truck drivers struck for a pay bump from $2,820 to $3,540 yearly. In 1978, a year *before* they struck, NOPD received a 63% pay increase, their salaries jumping from $6,360 to $10,344. This wasn't just about money. Mostly white cops felt attacked by the respect sanitation workers won via union recognition and modest wage gains.

Not every cop strike succeeded. In 1978, New Orleans' first Black mayor, Ernest "Dutch" Morial, a former civil rights activist, son of the Seventh Ward, a cigar maker, and a seamstress, brought in police chief James Parsons, who had reformed Birmingham, Alabama's department in the wake of the Eugene "Bull" Conner's vicious regime. Rank-and-file police resented the mayor for acting to make the department accountable against charges of corruption and misconduct. During the strike, officers "egged and vandalized the mayor's residence while yelling racial slurs." Some cops struck for white supremacy, using sanitation workers and the will of their Black mayor as indices for what this supremacy meant.

Ultimately, Morial helped turn public-opinion against the striking police by placing blame for the cancellation of Mardi Gras squarely on the police's shoulders. The cops didn't get the contract they wanted. Didn't get to be raised above sanitation workers (except for the money, the huge pay gap they enjoyed).

1970s to the Present: While cops went on strike using sanitation workers as a measuring stick for their own value, many city administrations responded to sanitation worker militancy by privatizing trash services. It is more difficult for the sanitation workers of one municipality to fight back against national and sometimes international corporations such as Waste Management, Inc.

In response, some radical municipalists such as Cooperation Jackson's Kali Akuno have suggested breaking up huge city waste-collection contracts into smaller agreements so they are available to local waste-disposal operations and cooperatives. This drive toward more, smaller contracts would be concurrent with city programs that fostered the creation of cooperative workplaces. Akuno's goal for Jackson, Mississippi, is to put Black workers back in control of their city, its resources, and its services.

2018

In 2018, China implemented a policy that effectively turned back the importation of millions of tons of "recyclables," largely from the United States. China's garbage blockade relocated dioxin pouring from industrially worked plastics to the tailpipes of incinerators in towns like Chester, PA where tons of Philadelphia's trash burns.

Terrible consequence. But who can blame China for returning container ships full of wounded oxygen? Who can blame Chester's people if they begin their own garbage blockade? The snake of Philly's disposal chain will continue to writhe.

 | | ROUGH MUSIC

As more ppl enter the disposal chain, their potential power grows "if
        only you
knew how much useless waste / gave rise to verse" Akhmatova
        some poison
or its trace a survival strategy against the pure minded Inspiring
revulsion as an asset though

mixture as Wendy Trevino writes is in the actual a given and
celebrations of "impurity" can be a blinder
white people wear in their drive to
erase their need to understand
difference in the ideal
of mixture

and this essay Jake invited me to write is the easy stuff is in no way
        a solid relation w/anyone which
 is the real work Listening to a podcast
        while washing dishes,
D. Harvey suggests America has colonized the idea of freedom

84

1978-1981

At least one historian of ink says the first writing tool must surely have been carbon. Carbon was certainly proceeded by piss and shit, that ephemeral ink, first and last resort.

My father told me a story of someone who wrote his name in shit in the lobby of the building housing the agency that had recently fired him. I thought this was crazy. Later, I'd learn it was desperation to be heard. How do you get the state to listen? What do you got?

The 1978–1981 Dirty Protest by prisoners of the Irish National Liberation Army involved male prisoners and female prisoners refusing to leave their cells to wash or use toilets. The Dirty Protests are exceptionable in the annals of collective prisoner protest, according to Begoña Aretxaga, whose account this follows.

The Dirty Protests evolved out of a cycle of discipline and resistance that began with the INLA prisoners' refusal to wear prison uniforms after they had been reclassified from political to ordinary prisoners, an administrative move meant to delegitimize their political reality. In response to prisoners refusing their shirts (and wearing blankets instead), the prison administration disciplined them hard. In addition to beatings and 24/7 confinement, prison officials exercised control over the prisoners' waste-making. Prisoners' access to toilets was controlled by guards who could delay or deny it at will. Eventually, the administration made the prisoners move outside of their cells without their blankets—naked. They were also subject to frequent body searches in which guards would insert a finger into prisoners' anal cavities then into their mouths, noses, hair, and beards.

The protestors' response was to no longer seek the guards' permission to use their bodies. They began to dispose of their own waste through windows and door peepholes. When those were boarded shut, they disposed of their waste in the corners of rooms. When guards began to smear prisoners' mattresses and blankets in excrement during cell searches, they denied guards the satisfaction of performing this torture by smearing their own waste on their cell walls.

The press was not sympathetic to the Dirty Protest. That women participated—meaning menses was part of the protest—was particularly unfathomable to them. They described prisoners as having descended into savagery and madness, which satisfied English biases of Irish subjects. Amnesty International would describe their conditions as "self-inflicted." Sympathy would have to wait until their hunger strikes began in 1981, after, for some, a decade of imprisonment.

There are important, nuanced political, sociological, and psychoanalytical paths to stalk here. Begoña Aretxaga, from whom I've heavily borrowed for this account, does. The Dirty Protests are also part of the fabric of centuries of Irish struggle against English imperialism. I'd like to emphasize a literal fact: in refusing to let the guards rule their shit and their orifices, the prisoners forced the guards to deal with it, to live with the vibrant misery of someone else's filth. The prisoners' actions involved extreme discomfort to themselves, but it also snared their captors in this misery while trying to signify to observers their abject conditions, to write it on the walls.

The Dirty Protests risked a great deal. The message and medium crowd and radiate. Bystanders have to read between their eyes and nose. The world chose to see the Dirty Protest not as a sign of their captors' cruelty but as an insane stunt by the prisoners.

In the borderlands of Texas, ICE force-fed prisoners on a hunger strike via a tube through their nostrils and down their throats. When are you reading this? What is the right tense for this sentence? "Force-fed," "are force-feeding," "will continue to force-feed"? Where is this place? In the borderlands of Texas? Across the national archipelago of immigration jails and camps?

A swathe of Australia as big as some states burned, a billion animals were estimated dead, 400 million tons of carbon were released by the inferno. The people of island nations like Kiribati are slowly evacuating among rising tides and increasing flooding, trying to avoid cultural death in that evacuation or deportation back to the threatened island. States force prisoners to fight fires intensified by climate change. Indigenous people of Bolivia are enduring a far-right coup and crackdown, not unrelated to capitalists' desire to secure the nation's lithium deposits for the emerging market for green technology in the Global North. Journalists do the work of real estate developers by positioning cities like Buffalo as climate change refugees, adding fuel to the fires of the speculative housing market, intensifying the pace of the displacement of working-class households of color.

You know this: capitalists are committed to the plantationocene, an uneven climate apocalypse—uneven in that it is marginalized populations whose labor was and is super-exploited in producing commodity landscapes/tombstone grids. Many of these marginalized people suffer and will continue to suffer a toasting world's worst effects. In any transition to a green economy, there is a real risk these populations will be coerced into bearing the costs of these transitions while being excluded from its benefits. A green future can still take place on a plantation. A green future can be fascist.

Anna Lowenhaupt Tsing lemme know that the metabolism of capitalism can no longer be shut down at a few crucial points of production. To a large degree, capitalism has achieved the dream of liquid production. Lead companies can afford armies of professionals to translate vernacular knowledge into industrial processes, to translate marketing slurry into local idioms, to slide consumption practices along the grain of cultural norms. Lead companies can move extraction, production, and laborers within states and across national borders with relative ease. They can also collaborate with states to create and deliver into the processes of production of racialized super exploitable populations or develop AI to do the production and leave to the workers the always brutal tasks of raw extraction or waste remediation. Capital is increasingly fluent in translating between links of the supply chain, replacing links that are sites of resistance, and turning heterogenous cites of production into uniform inventory. That is, corporations don't make, they expropriate, coordinate, brand, and purge.

If, while the world burns, the point of production can change, then, many suggest, distribution systems are weak points in capitalism's metabolism: UPS, FedEx, docks, rail, and air workers, truck routes, and distribution warehouses. The workers who make movement can shut down huge sectors of economic activity. This is why there is so much attention to the dramas of Amazon workers and UPS Teamsters (recently again sold out by their anti-democratic union). Or the idea that the threat of flight-attendant strike combined with an informal air traffic controller sickout ended a federal shutdown. The AFA (Association of Flight Attendants) has had some marvelously militant peaks.

on highways, driverless cargo haulers and stacking cranes in shipyards--because it means automating elements of distribution. Counter to technological utopian thought, automation will only displace labor, creating segregated zones where what is left to the human is intensive consumption and segregated zones for the most brutal forms of material and affective disposal labor.

So I also look toward the distribution chain's double: the disposal chain, the sink network, the makers of oblivion.

I want the history of lurching waste flows and accumulation, the labor of carriage and decomposition, the production of intensified difference and hierarchy among workers, and the rebellions of those laborers: Mudlarks; dirt-carters; loaders of horse-corpse barges, dung ships, and containerships; workers in ship-breaking yards; emotional garbage sorters and haulers. What if it was a celebrated labor? To disassemble the titans.

Climate change is destroying or will destroy the world many of us recognize. It has already driven species into the community of extinction. Another thread sliced from the web of life. When crucial threads go, the web of life may fold and fall.

Beyond trading carbon credits, the grossest fantasies of rolling back the plantationocene prioritize remediating the carbon already in our atmosphere, translating trillions of tons of atmospheric pollution into something benign. To sniff the value in the waste, to turn it into a product for the market. A shower of coins on a parade of silver bullets: carbon sequestration, pumping CO_2 back into the earth, etc. etc, etc.

There is no hell, no bottomless hole in which to stuff waste. No place that waste does not eventually escape. O ontological fantasy. Like recyclables in a clean blue bin incinerated into the sky. The oceans, the skies, the stomachs of mountains, the filtering organs of our bodies, our emotional cores. They break. They rupture.

These schemes are attractive because they don't make structural changes to assemblages of energy production and consumption. Rather, they find an alternative disposal method, a different sector of the planet to turn into a carbon dump, different ecologies, and people to put to work metabolizing the waste of the carbon economy.

What might a garbage strike look like on a planetary scale? What would it demand?

Upstate the barn they own a farm *farm*
own a commodity landscape/plantation Barn
trailer in the background Everyone else in town
working one side of the prison Working the upstate
milker at 2 AM whose kid from the Plantationocene/
lower peninsula/commodity landscape forced
or super-exploited Farm, legally less than minimum
or w/o any right A root criminalization of non-whiteness
of immigration a root devaluation of feminized & reproductive work
  violent exclusion
from wage enough for life Barn, Plantationocene displacement
   & erasure
of first ppls colonists' waste speech prepares the ground
for theft Farm, for colonists' waste speech turns ecologies in glamour,
  in their exchanging
changes ppl buries dense fabrics of use Farm turns excess
to waste the pleasure of snap
of opaque polysyllabic law's bulldozers
Terra Nullius (land belonging to no one) wasteland underutilized slum
Empty *Hactenus Inculta* (hitherto uncultivated) unproductive *Terra*
Incognita (unknown land) excessive, *Res Nullius* (nobody's property)
  & power
so excessive in and of itself sees waste as
the halo the powerless wear: Anarchic, communist
or socialist direct participation excess

The militarization of the police partly the military solving a problem
        of disposal equipment
obsolesced in the endless arc of imperial wars and the will
to wage imperial wars endlessly Downcycled ethnostate
Letter written in uranium dust on the toilet stalls of the Pentagon
        Letters of lead
pipes spelling "Rick Snyder" half-buried in his vacation
home lawn hundreds of miles from Flint
Imagined: the relentless crafty Lavatory Attendants Assembly Love
        Canal council
search Isidro Gutierrez, Lubbock, TX, 1968 work w/no
uniform, gloves, boots, or drinking water One Green New Deal
would eviscerate the military another would find
a carbon-neutral way of killing people
living their only lives over rare-earth deposits
while celebrating the women CEOs of bomb makers One Green
New Deal only passes with a Gray deal that pays
people to gather information about their friends and make
threatening calls
to strangers: full employment?
Full unemployment
Nothing is liquid
nothing is light

Bluewhale concretion
of lipids, wet wipes etc fatberg threatened to stop
the sewer system Workers spent
almost two mo. hack w/ shovels,
hoses Object of work 1/6 of a year, 1/400 of life
into biodiesel Shamecam installs
state explainers on

Londoner's bad disposal habits not the hurricanes' private
jets shit Huge honeycombs of Youtube,
Pornhub Facebook accretions of planets of content
100,000 waste workers (perhaps half SM employees) grind
shifts through gore (human, animal) Nazi humor
image factory corrosion
outsourced to the Philippines or American
dorms for less pay no support The censors
decide in seconds to go home with an unrelenting load of toxic
posts erupt in their sleep often NDA-ed

can't RT the poison
unshakeable Pays
better than most I dream
Paul Hollywood's widening maw around
a cake that plays a beheading
clip seasoned w/salt salt salt
salt salt What's a content mod

strike? What's ambiguous enough trash to
get you to linger? From experience metaphor
for affective work jumping up and down on dumpstered
seedlings to squash in more seedlings "Biocide
Application: Do Not Enter. Do Not Remove Sign for 24 Hours"
            Poison
party, marked like this free

in the lobby's sheen
if destruction of the property of the state is punished as murder
what if that property began to murder
the oppressive wings of the state
in body, mind, or spirit to auger into or relocate
returning waste to its maker

to begin the contamination of their works
one can't rest dripping w/shit

Gravediggers will not bury
the dead no one will show
to digest the steaming dead
they will remain in sight unattended
Utopic demand trucks go
uncovered again or w/clear body
the garbage of everyone
on parade and the grief
of those positioned as dumps
for others' bad feelings can be grief
out and out, anger attended
in light of its purpose

And that rare healing thought pulsing in these threads outside of my
    power fantasies what is it?

Does even talking in terms of waste let neoliberalism set the terms of
    the debate?
At the factory I put defective books into a crusher
I put this in the crusher

press a green button and watch it die Most books go the same born
under the factory's false stars boxed warehoused then pulped Writing
that seeks immortality lives ironic life

Desire often circulates between oneself and the libraries of mostly
        fucked up institutions
Phrase's week-long life having accomplished its end

occluding a jet causing waste to soak
private wealth This may not be hard A quiet gesture in a quiet place A
        tube sock full of corn starch flushed into the guts
of some bad house after one has exhausted other recourse sparks joy
        Haven't said
I've been successful at it better at denying my sadness "a
        garbage disposal

worker lives 15 years less than
any other worker, and we are 3 times more likely
to die before reaching age 65," said CGT's Baptiste Talbot,
Paris 2018.

2020

March 24, 2020, Covid-19: lockdown or quarantine for some, for others a dangerous public weather. Pittsburgh: city sanitation workers walk off the job and block city buildings with their trucks. A wildcat strike by Teamsters Local 249. They wanted PPE. They weren't getting it. Instead, their bosses asked them to sign a form saying they had been tested for Covid. They had not. The sanitation workers wanted safety; their bosses wanted to manufacture its administrative illusion.

Crisis is a sort of new sun. It's light at a different spectrum, its position and incandescence
revealing the striations of surfaces remained smooth, throwing into relief the cracks in what seemed whole.

In hospitals, clinical waste piles and piles. In households, worn-out PPE, tissues, intimately touched matter piles and piles. On one day, February 24th, the city of Wuhan produced 200 tons of medical waste. In the United States, these numbers are difficult to come by. No surprise. Either way, sanitation workers bubble lives by removing that vivid matter our bodies shed. They assemble a sort of shadow-polity—the landfill—where we mingle less than six ft apart.

In modern United States sanitation labor actions, workers often demand things so necessary and inexpensive it's almost unbelievable sanitation companies don't provide them in the first place. In 1968, in Lubbock, TX, Isidro Gutierrez and fellow, striking sanitation workers, mostly Mexican-American, had to demand uniforms, gloves, and drinking water. Without department-provided uniforms, the work destroyed their clothes. Without water in the West Texas heat, they were forced to drink from hoses in yards. Without toilets at the landfill, they were forced to go behind piles of garbage. Respect, safety, money: strike. The story was similar but not identical to many civil rights era sanitation strikes. See St. Petersburg. See Memphis.

As Wendi C. Thomas' historical journalism reminds us, the 1968 Memphis Sanitation Strike involved a public works department whose white management refused to protect its Black workers from the conditions of their work. A city policy forced garbage collectors to take refuge in bad weather in the backs of the trucks, where garbage was fed into the compactor. The policy killed two workers on Feb 1, 1968, when on an "especially rainy Thursday afternoon, city sanitation workers Echol Cole and Robert Walker took shelter in the back of a garbage truck when it malfunctioned." Their deaths precipitated the strike where MLK took his labor turn.

Sheldon White in Pittsburgh 2020: "We want better equipment, better protective gear, we have no masks." The Pittsburgh Post-Gazette reports one worker claiming "The gloves they currently use don't protect their hands and allow water and liquids to drain down inside."
Gloves that work, a thin layer of plastic, a tight weave of fabric, space between the self and refuse, Covid-19 or not. Sanitation workers die and are injured at some of the highest rates of any worker in America that gets counted.

Supervisor: You check in yet?
Moss: Yes sir, I did.
Supervisor: Go out to your route.
Moss: I'm not doing that.

What equipment do Pittsburgh's sanitation workers want? Puncture-proof gloves, masks, heavy-duty boots, hand sanitizer, and distancing policies, according to labor officials. What are they getting? Sometimes nothing. Sometimes pathetic gestures, like one facemask and two boxes of nitrile gloves for 35 trucks. Sometimes policies that steamroll their concerns. OSHA (utterly captured): "Workers and employers should manage municipal (e.g., household, business) solid waste with potential or known COVID-19 contamination like any other non-contaminated municipal waste." OSHA makes no distinction between the PPE workers should receive for municipal and medical waste. Waste workers don't get even that. A Pittsburgh sanitation worker would die of Covid-19 in mid-April. It was officially reported that the man "did not contract the virus while at work." I doubt this was any consolation to those who worked with him as they remain unprotected from the virus through the material they handled and unprotected from the virus through each other.

WHITE WINGS STRIKERS APPEAL TO MAYOR GAYNOR

Riots Renewed All Over the City When New Drivers Start Out to Clean Streets Under Escort of Police.

With mobs assaulting and stoning drivers and policemen all over the city and with miles of streets piled high with decomposing refuse, Strike Organizer William H. Ashton proposed an armistice to Mayor Gaynor this afternoon, providing the Mayor will consent to appoint a committee of citizens to hear the grievances of the striking Street Cleaning Department drivers.

11 Nov 1911 *The Evening World*. It starts like this: "With mobs assaulting and stoning drivers and policemen all over the city and with miles of streets piled high with decomposing refuse." Describing scabs and cops setting out to clear the streets:

Inspector Cahalane sent twenty-five men up on the nearby roofs, where they found hundreds of men and boys, and not a few women, hiding behind cornices with their arms filled with bottles and brickbats. They were driven into the tenements and the procession of carts went unscathed until they turned into Market Street. Then suddenly from the roof of No. 56 Market Street there rained down a shower of chimney cornices and bricks. Half a dozen drivers were picked off their carts, and as soon as they could scramble to their feet they fled. Several drivers were forced to seek shelter under their carts.

Both the mounted and foot policemen were struck by missiles and compelled to send reinforcements. Ten strike-breaking crews quit right there and the five that continued on to Park Row and Worth street passed through a dozen more showers of stone, wood, and fragments of concrete.

I HATE THAT YOU DIED

I HATE THAT YOU DIED

To hear you sing, turn
the stream, to hear you
folding silence, letting
silence touch
silence between the
burning manifold of yr
glowing thru the subzero
curb and drifts
escaping sleep, awake
in its awakening
among the mostly
empty and stackable
chairs, for he was
/
worse than
dead, he was confused
and vomiting half
heartedly on the tile
in the stall, an idea
w/o ppl, the song, void
and empty day, dull
same and song, void split
shift split where sleep
my better spirit spoke
turned edges refract

light still the splits shift
so I sleep less, output
more, hope and buy
my life back later, dig up
my shadow a boss killed
/
the angel of this waste
dumper is not the an-
gel, I am the angel
sweeping this plaza
by 7 am moonlight
is a river
sick w/drowning angels
/
as the sun's warm tongue
licks February ice
melt soaking as if
the world were cereal
bullshit, soft as it is
what you lost, what I lost
what we lost though each loss
differs though both losses
hurt each hurt differs I
mean why isn't holding
each other working why
can't we walk through
the gate of this hurt together

the light is going out but
just in one eye
why can't we walk together
through this gate, this hurt
/
I mean a river sick
w/drowning angles is
3rd job mopping down
a bar moonlight
a river sick w/drowning
angels, my little words, where are
you? where did you go? who
kept you, too long, too
who mouthed you w/small
intentions? I take you back,
little words I want
/
to drown my desire to
destroy my desire to
drown this is your sickbed
I'm leaving a review
to show me you could
kill me I swung the
hammer you swung at
my head I don't
want to die I wasted
so much life

what else
/
would it be
each silence
generally silence
despair, submission
or belief that one is
only worth what they've
paid, to have a voice,
to sing until my throat is raw
each word's vibration
scours the next word, the song
song and song, piling clouds
in the skull of a mouse
trade my ketchup ration
for a search allowance
sweet ache of scarcity
the librarian tells
me it's time to go
I know I can return
to it all in my mind
like the king who let
us pull away gold letters
knotted to his doublet
when we pulled we made the
alphabet that made him
king, the alphabet we

trade for silence
stuffed into a hole
your lifeless body
is not a signifier
it is a dead body
it takes language to
tell you this so what I
don't care I don't care it
doesn't prove anything
Jesus' insurance was great
kill me when I'm dead
you just worked, read
/
the news: yr dead, I look
at the page, grow
broken at the root
you change too fast
time swims faster than I
reel it in, say it
at the gate, hello, sing,
you could and didn't
I remember that split
that silence that folding

THE WOUND

First, you want to light the candle. Then
I want to light the candle, to make the world
this small—at midnight. The axis
of the week one burning
thought. A little ball

of myrrh released.
I've learned each lesson

too late. What does the candle say?
 "Look at me."

/

This book says, "Let it burn."
I can't love those who say
"Let it burn." I don't love
who I was. Lying down in the dark
memory of the day
to watch a video a friend recorded
with a hundred beautiful strangers
singing, "Shut it down." How fine
the line between shut
and burn.

The screen dissolves.
Cheryl is not yet home.
Accuracy without ambition
is all I can ask for
from a poem.

George Oppen wrote in "Discreet Series," "Rooms outlast you." Pithy. And also indicative of a relation to time that is modest, sobering. We die, apartments go on. Their floors get scratched by someone else's chairs. Their vents fill with the dust of someone else's life. But those rooms also go, demolished to make way for some other, pricier structure. Or those rooms are split open by moisture and creatures seeking shelter in a zone of divestment. A frame of time in which things live decades to centuries.

When I was thirty-two, I saw the green thread of a seedling peeking out of a tub drain. A tangle of my partner's hair and coconut oil shampoo held the seed in the drain where it was rinsed by our showers. I squatted in the shower, pulled the plug of hair and seedling, then held this assemblage in my naked, damp hand.

Where did the seed come from? I had been eating flax seeds with my oatmeal. This one must have escaped the coffee grinder and my teeth, traveled, placidly, through yards of my intestine, and, because of its glutinous hull, got stuck in the hairs of my dank parts after a shit until I showered.

My consumption had failed to destroy. That which was shit was already blooming.

This drain seedling was my small window into a pre-modern world of fast-cycling matter. One's refuse didn't always travel far—dinner scraps shot back to life from the heap. Though the majority of people and things lived short lives, they also sometimes lived short and public afterlives. It would not be strange to think that what was lost or tossed would return or the thread of its life would wind its way into a different vessel. If time, endurance, were weight, before and alongside industrial modernity many things must have seemed light.

And if life didn't last, what endured was its medium—soil. A renaissance master gardener: "There is nothing but what may serve to amend that Earth or Soil returning to it by way of Corruption, under whatever Figure it returns to it . . . .all manner of Stuffs, Linnen, the Flesh, Skin, Bones and Nails of Animals, Dirt, Urines, Excrements, the Wood of Trees, their Fruit, their Leaves, Ashes, Straw, all manner of Corn or Grains, & c."

Rooms outlast us. But the contents of an already unresellable cell phone will outlast the room. It will also outlast most soils. Petroleum-based polymers will take their place alongside the mineral, exerting their own kind of geology. A geological force that may outlast the assemblages of power that birthed it, long after they boil themselves to death through carbon emissions.

Given that we, flesh, are affiliated with so many polymer immortals, I would like to suggest we imagine future time as present weight in order to see the world. If long after our bodies die, the case of a cell phone lives on into the thousands of years, its mass multiplied by (all that) time, would be unliftable. It would break your floors.

Our world is full of things swirling with the potential and marvelous mass of asteroids. And these things will become particles of long-chain polymers, rinds of code, and electronics turned leachate, chemistries spilling across virtual and material borders, attenuated bacteria and fungi blooming in subterranean, oceanic, and tropospheric masses. New ecologies.

Karen Brodine, the great socialist-feminist+, typesetting poet wrote,

make your hands move quickly on the keys
fast as you can, while you are thinking about:

the layers, fossils. the idea that this machine she controls
is simply layers of human work hours frozen in steel, tangled
in tiny circuits, blinking out through lights like hot, red eyes

As long as our labor is lost to ourselves and those we would be in solidarity with, might these tangles of junk be our final purgatorial vessel. That is, as long as we labor in normal time and do not—or cannot—enter revolutionary time (or maybe we should call it solidarity time). Foam of an office chair, a name tag, some pounded on keys, this doc perpetually reanimated by the energy of an archive—our hot, red eyes mute, frozen except for the slow blink of consciousness to a poet like Brodine.

And capitalists will work future generations into these geologies of human residue.

From Xie Xiangan's great poem (and title) "Production, in the middle of Production, is soaked by Production":

> In links
> by deep links
> deeper and deeper links
> then I'm baffled by the light
> I'm a railroad tie under the light

This is not a pop-up for organic farming, metal straws, or a compost theology but toward an understanding of the distributions of endurance and force. This is to say we're constantly shedding 10,000-pound nails, sweating out ponds of oil, shitting forests. Imperfectly aligned with capitalist production, a thumb over the hose, a wild chaotic force and an orbit that we can channel into open-ended projects of opposition and solidarity. Solidarity? Dario Azzellini in Communes and Workers' Control in Venezuela: "an open category, constituted in struggle which people can join."

I dream of the time when it is the red hot eyes of executives and cops looking out from rubble, the decommissioned salvage yards where the liquidators no longer get to enjoy oblivion or put their name on monuments substituted for public goods. Rather, the liquidators are finally frozen in the rubble, stuck as the mute and frustrated ghosts of a savage time.

ABOUT GARBAGE STRIKE

Garbage Strike was composed in early 2019 in the Industrial and Labor Relations library at Cornell University in Ithaca, NY. It was revised in April 2020 in Buffalo, NY. Its composition followed the employee's access to research materials and the poet's intuition to look at the one thing that is always at hand—waste—and its place in collective struggle.

In terms of the content of Garbage Strike, the researcher must now sweep up after the poet. Garbage Strike is meant to be suggestive; it grew from a small archive of peoples' insurgent imagination in relation to waste. It's not thorough historical scholarship, and I remain a student of the subject.

The moments Garbage Strike describes and its actors belong to their times and places. People figured out the horizon of what they could do with each other and what they had. Some of the struggles referenced were class struggles, some were anti-racist, some were anti-imperial. Often, in their contexts, these things couldn't be split from each other. Other times, they could. In the case of the Dutch carters, their strike had a terrible outcome: a cross-class compromise to exclude Black workers from that labor market, contributing to their treatment as super-exploitable workers.

As recent scholars like Charisse Burden-Stelly have persuasively theorized the operations of racial capitalism in the modern US context, new directions for the work open up. For instance, to seek more on-the-ground facts about these struggles and to understand their relation to the operations of racial capitalism through the contexts those facts provide. To learn to recognize how particular individuals and institutions translate the dynamics of racial capitalism into distributions of waste, hierarchies of labor, and extraction of profits—and the multifarious ways people get together and fight back.

Garbage Strike & Polymer Meteor /// Sources, direct & indirect.
Some read in an oppositional fashion.

Akuno, Kali. "Build and Fight: The Program and Strategy of Cooperation Jackson." Ed. Nangwaya, Ajamu. *Jackson Rising: The Struggle for Economic Democracy and Black Self-Determination in Jackson, Mississippi*. Montreal, Quebec: Daraja Press, 2017. 1-41.

Azzellini, Dario. *Communes and Workers' Control in Venezuela: Building 21st Century from Below*. Boston, MA: Brill, 2016.

Brodine, Karen. *Woman Sitting at the Machine, Thinking: Poems*. Seattle, WA: Red Letter Press, 1990.

Burnet, Thomas. *The Sacred Theory of the Earth*. London: Walter Kettilby, 1684.

Burrows, Edwin & Mike Wallace. *Gotham: A History of New York City to 1898*. New York: Oxford University Press, 1999.

Chen, Adrien. "The Laborers Who Keep Dick Pics and Beheadings Out of Your Facebook Feed." *Wired*, 10.23.14.

Cooper, Tim. "Recycling Modernity: Waste and Environmental History." *History Compass* 8/9 (2010).

De La Quintinye. *The Compleat Gard'ner*. Trans. John Evelyn. London: 1676.

Fernández, Johanna. *The Young Lords: A Radical History*. Chapel Hill, NC: University of North Carolina Press, 2000.

Gabrys, Jennifer. Digital Rubbish: A *Natural History Electronics*. Ann Arbor, MI: University of Michigan Press, 2011. https://www.press.umich.edu/973473/digital_rubbish

Hodges, Graham Russell. *New York City Cartmen, 1667-1850*. New York: New York University Press, 1986.

"How Strike Engulfed Britain in Trash: Mountains of Garbage, Half-Treated Sewage in Rivers, and other Health Menaces All Added to London's Plight after Public-Service Men Went on Strike." *U.S. News & World Report*, 11.16.70.

Hurl, C. "From Scavengers to Sanitation Workers: Practices of Purification and the Making of Civic Employees in Toronto, 1890-1920." *Labour/Le Travail* 79 (2017): 81-104.

McCartin, J. A. "'Fire the Hell out of Them': Sanitation Workers' Struggles and the Normalization of the Striker Replacement Strategy in the 1970s." *Labor: Studies in Working-Class History of the Americas* 2:3 (2005): 67–92.

McNeilly, John. *The St. Petersburg Sanitation Strike of 1968: a Process in Political Empowerment*. Thesis, Eckerd College, 1989.

Meilan, Solly. "You Can Now Watch the Whitechapel Fatberg's Decay on Livestream." *Smithsonian.com*, 8.16.18.

Moore, Sarah A. "The Excess of Modernity: Garbage Politics in Oaxaca, Mexico." The Professional Geographer, 61:4 (2009): 426-437.

Murphy, Michael Warren, and Caitlin Schroering. "Refiguring the Plantationocene: Racial Capitalism, World-Systems Analysis, and Global Socioecological Transformation." *Journal of World-Systems Research* 26:2 (2020): 400–415.

Palmer, Charles Steven. "'I'm Tired of Feeling like a Garbage Man': Labor, Politics, Business, and the 1978 Memphis Fire and Police Strikes." Ph.D Dissertation., The University of Mississippi, 2002.

Romero, Yolanda G. "Adelante Compañeros: The Sanitation Worker's Struggle in Lubbock, Texas, 1968-1972." *Texas Labor History.* Ed. Bruce Glasrud and James Maroney. College Station, TX: Texas A&M University Press, 2013.

"Sanitation Workers Begin Strike in New Orleans." New York Times, 1.21.1969.

Tsing, Anna Lowenhaupt. *The Mushroom at the End of the World: On the Possibility of Life in Capitalist Ruins.* Princeton, NJ: Princeton University Press, 2015.

Xiangen, Xia. "Production in the middle of Production, is soaked by Production." *Iron Moon: An Anthology of Chinese Worker Poetry.* Ed. Qin Xiaoyu. Trans. Eleanor Goodmna. Buffalo, NY: White Pine Press, 2017.

Yépez, Heriberto. *The Empire of Neomemory*. Translated by Jen Hofer. Oakland, CA: ChainLinks, 2013.

"White Wings Strikers Appeal to Mayor Gaynor: Riots Renewed All Over the City When New Drivers Start Out to Clean Streets Under Escort of Police." *The Evening World*, 11.11.11.

Wiggington, Michael Peter et al. "Hold That Line : The New Orleans Police Strikes." *Criminal Justice Review*, 26:3 (2015): 234-251.

Zhang, Hao, and Eli Friedman. "Informality and Working Conditions in China's Sanitation Sector." *The China Quarterly* 238 (2019): 1–21.

Poems from this MS appeared in *Afternoon Visitor, Anvil Tongue Books, Apartment Poetry, Best Buds! The Buffalo News, Collective, Elderly, Ethel Zine, Here, Homestead Review, JMWW, PEN America Blog, Poetry Northwest, Snail Trail Press,* and *Sporklet.* They were also featured in the Buffalo Ochre Papers chapette *Moldy Donuts.* Thanks to the editors: TR Brady, Maggie Nipps, D.C. Wojciech, Mike Walsh, Orchid Cugini, Bob Pohl, Nicholas DeBoer, Jamie Townsend, Sara Lefsyk, Joanna Penn Cooper, Jason Labbe, Maria Garcia Teutsch, CarlaJean Valluzi, Danniel Schoonebeek, Serena Solin, Woogee Bae, Danika Stegeman LeMay, and Edric Mesmer.

During the different stages of writing this book crucial encouragement, feedback, shelter, inspiration, or being with from these readers, correspondents, friends, and fighters was immense: The Annus Mirabilis Working Group, Simeon Berry, Jay Besemer, Marty Cain, The Catherwood Librarians, Allison Cardon, Jennifer Conner, Noah Falck, Fitz Fitzgerald, Robin Jordan, Brandon Lewis, Tim Liu, Kina Viola, Jake Reber, Derek Seidman, Sergio, Ryan Kaveh Sheldon, Jeremy Spindler, J. Hope Stein, Carra Stratton, Angela Veronica Wong. And, always, always, Cheryl Quimba. Thank you.